Animal Mothers
Atsushi Komori
Illustrated by Masayuki Yabuuchi

This edition is published by special arrangement with Philomel Books, a division of The Putnam & Grosset Group.

Grateful acknowledgment is made to Philomel Books, a division of The Putnam & Grosset Group for permission to reprint *Animal Mothers* by Atsushi Komori, illustrated by Masayuki Yabuuchi. Text copyright © 1977 by Atsushi Komori; English text copyright © 1979 by The Bodley Head; illustrations copyright © 1977 by Masayuki Yabuuchi. Originally published in Japan by Fukuinkan Shoten, Publishers, Ltd., 1977.

Printed in the United States of America

ISBN 0-15-302110-1

4 5 6 7 8 9 10   035   97 96 95

Animal Mothers

Atsushi Komori

Illustrated by Masayuki Yabuuchi

HARCOURT BRACE & COMPANY
Orlando Atlanta Austin Boston San Francisco Chicago Dallas New York
Toronto London

Mother cat carries her kittens
in her soft mouth.

Mother lion carries her cub in her mouth, too.

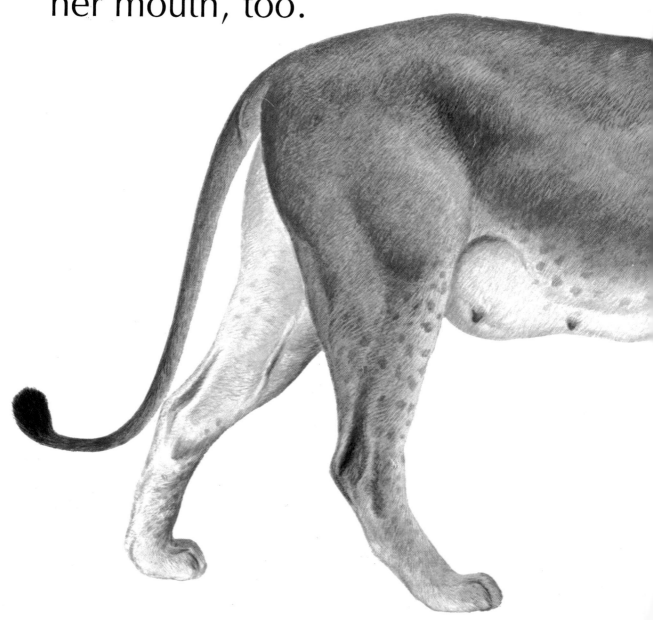

Mother baboon's baby clings tightly to her stomach.

Mother chimpanzee carries
her baby in her arms.

Mother koala's cub
rides on her back.

Mother sloth carries her baby on her stomach.

Mother kangaroo carries her joey in her pouch.

Mother elephant gently
pushes her baby with her
trunk to make it run.

The zebra foal runs along
behind its mother.

Baby wild boars follow their
mother all in a bunch.

Baby hedgehogs follow their mother in a nice straight line.

28